Fanatical Kink Poetics

By

Jamel Latria Daralea

ISBN: 1-4140-3271-4 (e-book)
ISBN: 1-4140-3272-2 (Paperback)

This book is printed on acid free paper.

1stBooks - rev. 12/09/03

CONTENTS

Thick and Thin

Soil

Essence of Me

You are filled with the very essence of me

Thy skin, thy blood

Thy bone, thy brain

Thy spirit and thy soul

What you are is who I am

And

Who I am is what you are

Trust and believe in me

Believe and trust in yourself

For there is no room in the lacking

We are like the sun and the moon

The light that brightens the day

To awaken the body

To appreciate nature

The melodious halo to soften the night

To rest the body

To comfort nature

Nevertheless, we are the same

We have a purpose

We are existence

Nature

Nature

I cannot help but think how marvelous the entity to put forth all this

beauty

And

Once this beauty had no flaws

Though now...

How blue the sky

With its thick clouds, like snow piles on a bright blue lake

Peaceful

How the wind swims over the trees

Dance they do, the leaves, changing colors and falling

Captivating

How the snow is so white and fluffy

How the grass is so green then brown

How the stars diminish in the day and then sparkle so bright in the

night

How the sun is overpowering

And

The moon so lazy

Back into the water

Back

Back

Into the Earth

The true maternal birth

Back

Back

Shut up!

Stay away

Leave me alone I say

It is they

Not me

I give you water and seed

I love and bleed

Honesty

I do say and believe

Earth don't want us you see

The heavens cry

It shrieks at our existence

Shame

Shame

We are

Adam and Eve's stupidity

Eat of the fruit

Food for the mind

The body

The soul

Shall I drown or dig my hole

Will I be reborn?

Molded from a deeper hole

I say as we die

And

People cry

At our paralyzed last sigh within our still protruded figures

Our spirits do lift and regain small mass

The universe shatters are spirits into stars

To float around the hot planet called Mars

I say our heavy bodies full of soul

Trash

Waste

Unneeded substance

Buried in the wood

The skins of the tree

We once stood between and peed

Puked

Shit

Climbed

Hide 'n' go seek

The flowers and grass

Poked and withered

Will live upon thee

Dissecting into every pore

To plant their roots

We took

So shall they

And the shame

That we abuse the very land that shall stand into our presence

Who shall open gates into our make believe stance of spirits and ghost

Our forever host, nature

My Country

I love you

My country

My maternal mother

My obedient sister

Thy molded dust that formed and structured my very being

Grew my food

Housed and cleansed me

That worships and conditions me into a man

That seduces and produces me into a woman

And

When I fall

Helps me stand

The strength and protection of my father and fathers

The love and care of my mother and mothers

The same love you shared with me

I love you my country

More than the blood, that flows beneath my skin

Heaven preserve us

All Africa

You are

Insatiable for praise

Jamel Latria Daralea

Blue Nile

Lying on the cool rocky surface of the Blue Nile

It caressing the side of my body with sudsy leftovers of small waves

My eyes squinting from the suns stare

The bitterness of browning onions and bebere all through the air

Mingling with incents

Roasting Buna and the popping of dry popcorn

Oh, and the laughter of the kids just a ways from me hopping around in

the shallow waters naked

The man with his beautiful voice

His voice to sound as sweet as the music that his fingertips brought

forth from the strings

Forever, tranquil memories

Berhanu my light that shines for me

All the light I wish to see

Berhanu thy light makes my beauty graceful

Red Sea

The warm silky touch of the Red Sea

Dripping off my toes

Sliding off the tips of my fingers as I made circles and waves

Round and round I go

This sea of ages

Priceless

Serene

Breathing about its sweet moist

Coming forth from the heat that burns in the air

I lie back against the hard

Warm

Rock

The grass pulling its pointy surface to scratch and tickle my skin

The boiling air separating a million times over in front of my eyes

I fall wickedly into the seduction that the Sea brings

The ancestry of years and years releasing from my thoughts into the

present

Walking along the calm flowing of the Red Sea

Washing the dirt from their feet into the blue green water

Washing their clothes of all their sins and all their strains

The women releasing into the water their menstrual pains

That it would hide them of there shameful and unbearable fluids

And

Bring back their beauty

Ah the Red Sea

Not red at all but of a muddy blue green

I am obliged to hold fast all that was and is on me

For it is the serenity of the Red Sea that massages my aggressions

Wakens my obsessions with the old and new

Its warmth and tease painting worlds before my eyes

Red Sea

America

The proud

The Just

The free

The land where she feeds but her people starve

Where the signs on billboards of two hands black and white

Stand tall over walls

However, the streets see all

The nerve to flower the stripes

Of red, blue and white

And all it's might

When centuries scream of stolen races

From far away places

The pain and anguish that logo many faces

Cultures lost and nobody cares

Communication is rare

The country leads a land of mockery

As the rich, get caviar, crab legs, and too much wine

And

Lost criminals get lucky serving time

The streets become elated with children

Families broken from the stress

Let the truth be heard

We fight wars that are yours

And

You dream of America

And

Wish to get away

Let it be known

The land of the free

The doped

The cheated

The land of the tears

The dreams and wasted years

The land of all races

Who still have no place

Freedom land

Understand

America Again

America the dream the dreamers dream

America the vision

America

For every star

Is ten thousand fold for the suffering

Yeah America

Though immigrants, aliens, foreign companions

Whatever

Hold fast to the hope of democratic equality

Of a homeland free for opportunity and wealth

Of broken chains and endless plains

And many cities of lights with definite plight

And so much plentitude

Though behind the flag of

Red, white and blue

Hide many fools

That welcomes servitude

Who lie and cheat

And

Hide centuries of pain

Blood stain, rusty chains

Branders and stolen fame

For their millions

However, this is our home

It leeched into our Indian bloodline, our Indian culture, our territories, and our serenity

It leeched into our African bloodline, our African culture, and our serenity

Crippled our culture and heritage, our truths and beliefs, who we were and could have been

A long time passing, for this pseudo-American dream

Built from my ancestors hands and broken backs

Who built America with prayer, song, and dance

And lost dreams on top of dreams for one dream

Equality

A future foreseen for you and I

Love Letter to Africa

The pain of birth

Oh does it hurt

It hurts thy womb

It hurts thy heart and soul

When birth becomes a curse

O sweet mouth of Africa

Open up and scream

Scream Africa

Scream your pain with rain

Scream for strong crops

And a lot of money

O large eyes of Africa open up and see

Your children suffer and their children

Your children bleed

O strong arms of Africa grab hold your continent

Why must you give up, Africa?

Flourish old mother and be kind

O legs of steel and gold stomp into the lands

Your diamond fingers scratch and bleed out the filth

and rebirth your lands clean

O generous mother, why are you selfish

Do you not see the curse?

Do you not feel the pain and anguish of your children?

Of your fighters

Of your mothers who bleed and give, birth just as you
once did
Only to loose
One of us is suffering, mother
All of us are suffering, mother
We suffer, you suffer mother
Mother you suffer and we suffer
Look at your people
Look at your countries
Look at your past
Spirits of the slave, be still
Flesh of my flesh be still
Blood of my blood be still
O beautiful, dark, unhappy mother, forgive
Look at your present
Wicked, rebels who ruin the lands to sand
Greedy, murderers, rapist, haters
Rid of them
O Africa
Make us free
O Africa
How you suffer

Eve's Spring Pain

I awaken and sing Eve's spring this glorious morning

A delight of beauty is reborn from cold confines

Heavens soft veil of rain

The suns amber stain, refreshing thy beauty again

I awaken and sing Eve's spring as my petals bloom of shades that show

how delighted and curious I can be

I awaken and sing Eve's spring even in the twilight hour

For underneath the stars sultry glare I shine

The mouths of Earth do not criticize me

It desires me

Caresses me

Nourishes me

It loves and perfects me again

I awaken and sing Eve's spring even as the winds scream blemish after

blemish against my beauty

The rain is cold and hard

The suns amber stain is pale and gloomy sunken back by the gray of the

clouds

Heaven's soft veil has passed me and hell is eager to chastise thee

I still sing Eve's spring

I sing Eve's spring in my last moments

When the stars glare sparkles on another

And

The suns stain is far away

Even the Earth does not caress my withered petals

My beauty is fading, now a soul to compose alone

In the remnants of Eve's spring

I sing Eve's spring pain in quiet confinements once again

'Til my beauty is renewed and I am again used and pursued

Life's View

Jamel Latria Daralea

Life

To look around this world day to day

To smile

To cry

To fuss

To fight

To live sinful

Godly we try

Then to sleep and die

To wonder why it is that we are here

To wonder about the creator of all

Through the drama

To wonder how we take a fall

Overall how we are similar and different

As we try to be happy, we ruin all

Life that we seek though, we have

The views

All mystery

Mystery we are

In this creation

A creation that we make more than it is

The tunnel we see lighted bright

The birds we hear singing tunes to us watching over us

Man has become all

Since before time they say

For they created the light of the day again they say

And the women as prey, and whores

Begot from the tree of sin and made night darker than it would ever be

Though to suffer, they do still

Life is a book

I am in it

So are you

And

In this book, you shall see yourself once again

For we enjoy the life of mystery

Life of fiction

Life of poetry

We live as imitators

Creators

Actors of every word written in the golden book

We live life's desires

Sensual is life

In all its beginning

Never ending

Life's views

We have perfected its story

And mutilated its meaning

Life

The News

The news we see is a constant reminding of the future

The future so close it is near

Near is now the present

The present now resembles rapture

Let me not awaken and be alone

Let me not be alone when taken into the wings of the present warmth

Police

You fools you think you rule

Wipe the drool from your badges

A badge of honor

A badge of disgrace

You badge wearing bully

Fool

Gun carrying idiot

Fool

Baton swinging street curser

Fool

Stride in your pride

Someone will have your hide

Fool

With your belly chafing

Rubbing up against your cheap leather belt

Devil

Punk

Weakling

Skunk

You go home to your wife

Eat, fart, and beat her ass

You swear at your kids and make them last priority

Fool

You do not fit in

Therefore, you corrupt within the system

And

When you die from the stride in your pride

The only ones in line outside the cathedral doors

Are the racist and whores

Partners and wives

Ex-cons on their sides

Your kids so relieved that they forget to cry

A devil following priest thinking about his 1910 gin

See you will never win

Tomorrow a new trainee to take over your seat

To replace your whack offbeat switch on the street

Damn

What happened to Officer Friendly?

Fool

Prison Song

He is sitting in his jail cell

Definitely aware that he will be old as hell

Before he will stare at the beautiful blue sky

Wider than the Lord can provide

And

That is if he can survive the prison butchers stolen kitchen knives

The prison guards crooked insight

The sexually depressed, mind regressed prisoners fondling their loins in

his ass

He is sitting in his jail cell living day after day

Creating colored wigs from his own pubic hair

Cutting a mini skirt from an old pillowcase

Have to be somebody's woman to escape a deadly fate

Trying to distant himself from realization of damnation and find Jesus

It is Heaven that he thinks of…

But he's going to hell

He has no fear, no fear at all, but strength

He was born free, yet he is not free

However, until he is free, he will not rest

Although rest will come in death for he, and still he will not be free

It is Heaven that he thinks of…

But he's going to hell

Thomas A. Dorsey wrote, *Take my hand precious lord…*

Yet as this prisoner sings this song of faith and will, his fingertips are

stale from

Rendezvousing with the steal on his cell

The breeze on his palms is not from fresh air of the Earth but it is from the swinging girth of his cellmates yearning

It is Heaven that he thinks of…

But he's going to hell

He is not sane

He is talking to the shadows on the cement walls

Becoming familiar with them all

Although there is one that he cannot come to terms

He yearns for freedom but his fingerprint burns a shadow of evil

With a strain and sigh he awakens every morning, wondering is this the day he will die

With a strain and a sigh he falls to his sleep wondering is this the night he will die

To be buried in the freedom for sale lot on the government plot

Ghetto

I do not know the ghetto

Not personally

I do not know

Only by what I see displayed

On the television

On the movies

The neighborhoods devouring its children deep into the potholes that

damage their streets

Deep into the waste

And

I do not know

The streets

The ghetto, dead but alive street

I do not know the promiscuity

Only the weaved women that stand alone

The white beat up

Black and blue whores

That smile there cummed stained, yellowish, brown teeth

Never less

I am not blind

I see the hoes with the dirty thugs, pimps

I see them giving head on the rug in your back seat

I do not know the ghetto

Sometimes I wish I did

Sometimes I wish I had

'Cause right now my life is bad

And

I am so damn naive

Under the suburban lights

I literally fight for my life

My black skin is a sin

My womanhood a slab of meat to men

And the white sneaky

Oh, do they pry

Wishing me bad luck

Those black faces that pass by

The numbers are getting high

Passing by my roses and mowed grass so green

The birds eating hard breads and seeds

They say (the blacks); sell out, to me, easily

They say (the whites), nigger! only to please their insanity

For me (the blacks), they litter their grins

They dance on my lawn with loudness and slang

For me (the whites), they complain

They exaggerate all my gains as if I am a criminal pain

They fight my property until it is destroyed

I do not know the ghetto

Nevertheless, it just feels like the ghetto wants me

Blood; I beg your pardon?

What kind of family am I in?

That I would wish the worst sin

For it all to end

Then maybe tomorrow I would smile a while

Take it all back and grin

However, it is blind for it hides beneath the skin

The wicked thoughts from within

The shame and the pain

Blood

Water

Blood thicker than water

I beg your pardon.

I wish to disagree

I wish to make a plea

To be free

Waters been good to me

Cleansed my skin way back when

The pimples popped white from my pores

Grew my hair silky thick

Washed my body of shame

The waters cool my fevers

Washes down the phlegm critters

The tobacco grinds in my lungs

That bitters my throat

Turns me from old to young

Never scorns my insides

Like the blood that is shared from you to I

From him to bride

From the bride to her hide I am bore

A woman who cares more for her panties

Deep down

She is tossed

From the hurt and the cost

And the years that she's lost

The hugs and the love

She needs the man up above

And in a man

Out a man

Her confusion a tear in her cycle

And

Thy children lie dormant in her cramps

The tan from the rays her eyes made

Darken up our lives

Masquerade around our childhood

A complete merry go round into our adulthood

Blood is thicker than water

Only skin-deep

What kind of family is this?

That I would wish and wish

That the stars do not miss

And

Lightning's strict dance would strike me

I love the rain

I have been crying all my life

I love the storms

They have blown me over

A curiosity

What kind of family am I destined to lead?

The one the stars forgot to grant me

Blood is thicker than water

Only skin-deep

False Uplifting

A sad woman always believes she is right

An angry woman will want to fight

And

In the end, it is only confusion

And

Pain

But

Free

To draw tears

To weep

However, to weep, one must feel the energy of pain, and then the tears

will rise from the soul

The pain is imprinted there

It swells until your whole being rises out with a howl

And the howl into a growl or scream

But tired

Of the swollen skin beneath your caved in space of thinness

Under your closed, soaked eyelids

The cramping in your chest even after rest

The sore throat, dry and barky

No room for sumptuary

To find your rough spot and blot

It

Out

But relieved

Of the pressure and stress

Nothing left

Not even rest

And

The best is yet to come for the time is running on

Breakfast

Lunch and dinner is gone

Your tears have caked upon your face

Judgment has left you in a bad place

And

You still have the rest of the day to let go and put a false smile on your

face

Homeless

Homeless

Yeah I am

Without a home

Without a bed

To lay my head

Without a decent meal

Generously fed

Without sex when I want it

When I need it

Want to be it

The wet shaky lover on my own sheets

Homeless

Yeah I am

Does not mean I have never had a home

I use to roam around my house naked

The winds brushing on my skin

I use to sleep the nights away

In my bubble bath

No longer bubbled

I use to eat when I wanted

Filling my stomach

With the television and music

Playing every station

Homeless

Yeah I am

But

It will not last long

Just another test

Of my beloved father

I am in a place I do not want to be

With rules to test my every nerve

With people who don't deserve

Nothing

With used everything

But

It is just a test of my beloved father

Because I know as long as I smile

Walk every mile

Keep my head up in holy style

He will deliver me with a gift

And

Homeless I will not be

Nope not me

Still Homeless

Misery and shame

Poverty and pain

No shelter from the rain or snow

So cold

So cold

Friendless and growing old

Like a used up rag that has no use

Sick and thin like a pole

No food but molded bread and vein sprouted potatoes from donated

sheds

Eyes see through me like nails scratching

And the giving heart

Yeah right

That is a start

But rare

And in despair

I no longer care

Just as you don't care, if I am even here

You do not see me that bum on the streets soaking in the rain

Covered up with soiled newspapers in the snow freezing cold

You do not see me the person standing long hours with signs

Begging and I'm ashamed

Damn straight, I am ashamed

But

I am here

When I am dead

There will be twice of me on these lonely streets

Colder than the nights sky

Thinner than a squinted, eye

And hungry

Color of War

What color is war?

War is the enemy

You kill me

I kill you

We kill each other

They are dieing!

Do you hear them screaming?

Do you hear them crying?

The faces on the burning dollar bills

The green occupied with white faces

They are screaming and crying beyond the grave

"No man is good enough to govern another man without his consent."

Did a white man say that so long ago?

Lies

Lies

Sterilized and refined

Plagiarized and exercised

Knowing but not knowing

But not knowing and yet knowing

That it is still a white lie

They are dieing!

Do you hear them screaming?

Do you hear them crying?

Everyone poor and tore down around this

Pseudo-American

Followers

Use to be leaders, European

World

Man, woman and child

Falling off the breast of this Earthly life

Their suckling is incomplete

They are passing away hungry and dehydrated

Bloody and annihilated

Living in hell

Only to go to hell

Echoes of their anorexic shadows fading with a reminder

A life for a life

The West is the devil incarnate, they say

A life for a life

The West use us as prey

A life for a life

One day they pray

Revenge today they scream

Do you hear them screaming?

Do you hear them crying?

The noises so deathly

Like a migraine's rapid pulse hard against the temples

And the air so dark with life after passing life

Going up like silent birds

The stench of their passage

Human waste gases remains

And

Still the fighting

Still the screaming

Still the crying

Still the dieing

And

A child hides under his mothers sagging breast, weeping

A father will drag his half-dead body across the swallowing soil

Wondering if he will ever come home in pieces or come home at all

But through it all

What remains?

What green remains?

Large or little

Occupied with white faces

Do you hear them screaming?

Do you hear them crying?

The worlds children falling off the of the tree of life

Can you give to charity please?

America will beg us

America will lure us

Broadcast with their pious crookedness

Feed the children, please

Whose parents we killed

Rebuild nations

We have torn down

Sure and then

Maybe a movie ten years from now

When many are dead

Lives are stole

Companies are sought

As much as possible is westernized

For sure, this is the way and the only way

Not!

"No man is good enough to govern another man, without that mans consent."

Well when we kill and bomb all that he has

And, all that he knows

To beg for his life will be our gift

Let the welfare lines get longer

What color is war?

Green

Occupied with white faces

Color of War II

I will ask again

Do you hear them screaming?

Do you hear them crying?

Back here in the sweet land of the free and rich

The homeless, with there homemade billboard signs, though they have no home

On the highways begging for a little change for beer and nicotine

And then the in debt persons winning the lottery, so easily, though they are still in debt

Cause that money is not tax-free

And

Still the riches land on the worlds map

People are starving

One hundred billion pounds of food to waste

35 million Americans hungry

Please

Picking up frozen bodies in the winter, homeless

Run away children selling their bodies, prostitutes

"No man is good enough to govern another man without that mans consent."

He should have said

Govern your own, and indulge in the fruits of your labor

Cause America has its eye on the prize, outside of its own shores

Is this why my tax dollars flourish to enter another door without even a minimum return

Their hands are dirty Uncle Sam

Our hands are dirty Uncle Sam

Your hands are definitely dirty Uncle Sam

And

I am tired of calling you uncle fool, stealing my tax dollars for this bull

Corrupting my mind for this bull

Unbalancing my time for this bull

We cannot waste time wiping blood

'Cause my hands and feet hurt like the dickens with all this non

rewarding labor you toss at me

We cannot waste time wiping blood, Sam

Our eyes are not just to see death

Do you hear them screaming

Our hands are not just to hold weapons

Do you hear them crying

Our feet are not just to run

Do you hear them screaming

Our hearts are not just to feel pain

Do you hear them crying

Crying tears of blood from mountains

Running on torn skinned up feet

Thirsty and hungry fighters in the white sands

Bodies in the sea

Bodies in the clouds

Bodies still clinging to there souls

Souls dragging eerie shadows

A fight for life

They have a meaning

A fight for rights

They pursue a purpose

Revenge

Freedom

A dream

What is ours?

That we remain first and third world continues to be barely a third

Why can't we share the extravagates of being free?

Of living life as you and me

Whom, might I remind you, would be in a lot of misery without the
third worlds company

Diamonds and gold from Africa, close to illegal

Lead and oil from the east, cheap

Computers and cars from the Asian industry

You see the greedy on the green, occupied with white faces will never be
pleased

No, see because servitude equals plentitude

Kiss there ass cause they are first class not you

Does not matter what you give but only what you get that is there motto

Be torn down and stay down, you shall not rise, that is the surprise on
the greedy green

They will take and take and you will see no wrong but when you need a
bit back

You will need to beg and then borrow and now it is time to take from
the greedy green occupied with white faces

Sam broadcast across the world lies

Sam broadcast across the world fear

Same old Sam crap from a use to be corn fed, hairy back

Sam, go back to the pigs you swine

Overworking this population into debt and then you send us off to our deaths

Damn shame army does not know why they will kill or why they will die

Just doing the evil deal civil service for his and her country

His country will enjoy a nice hot dinner while he fights

Her country will moan, hump, and sweat sexual enjoyment on fresh smelling linen as she hides in the desert sands of another mans land

His country will slobber into supportive pillows and awaken refreshed when he dies

Her and his country will cry on a flag, shoot barrels of smoke, and choke on song

While their, remains of life are only but that, red, blue and white on cotton creased sheets

I am sure in their fight for life

As they died a painful death, they saw the light of the stars

All fifty of them sparkling

What color is war?

Green occupied with white faces

And

I see no Indian on the greedy green

I see no Black on the greedy green

I see no Asian on the greedy green

I see no Mexican on the greedy green

The greens just occupied with white faces and the greens in all the white places

If

If life could be CD's of your favorite, music floating around like clouds

Easily to notice and hear and sing along

Passing us by like airy drip drops

If people could go and come as they please

With no tease

Hatred

Mockery

If life could be choosing your mates

Endless dates

No whores

No bait

Anyone of any race

If life could be romantic

Sensual

Sin after sin but no real sin accompanying

If life could be the cause for the erotic tastes

Numb and swollen places

If life could be giving birth to babies with wings

Angels from within

Come... angels out

If life could give you stretch marks but take them away with a mans

kiss

His blissful exquisiteness makes you more beautiful than a princess

That he could

Touch your raw tender flesh

Stretched out

Played out from that angel you give

And

All disfiguration disappears

If life gave us families of geniuses

So wealthy money did not exist

So intelligent and free

No emphasis

Not any

If we could breathe fresh air

Get along with the bears or wildlife just alike

If we could drink water from the sea

Clean`like crystal blue in a blonde-haired person's eye

If I could go on and on and on

My ifs would never end

If I could be this serene

Would I really be happy?

Thanksgiving

What am I happy for?

Grateful for

Thankful for

What am I blessed with?

Well

About now as I smell the simmer of the stews

The brewing of the cabbage and greens

The baking of the pies

The broiling and frying

Of Thanksgiving, feast

Forming clouds of its own

Sweet pheromones to delight my taste and hungry senses

About now as I look at the silky sea of blue greens and purple in the sky

And

How in admiration it sets in my eyes

How only a few birds fly by and sing

And the squirrels quietly waiting for a toss or two of some unneeded

food

And the willow tree so serene dances in the breeze

I admire the peace and tranquility

What am I happy for?

Grateful for

Thankful for

What am I blessed with?

Well

About now as I listen to the smooth beats of no other beat

The jazzy, sassy, loud, fancy, moving and grooving, saddening,

brightening, soulful elegance of my

People

I can picture our rainbow lifting higher and higher on this day

I smell the kitchens the air

I hear our voices everywhere

I see our smiles and our grace

This day of coming together

Being one

What am I happy for?

Grateful for

Thankful for

What am I blessed with?

Well

It would be the chance of living

When I wish I were dead

It would be the chance to sing as I always sing when I open my mouth

It would be the chance to succeed when I felt I have gone nowhere

It would be the chance to bare children, for I am lucky now and I do not

realize it

But most of all it would simply be to be

Blessed abundantly for living at all

Petals, Pedals

Petals

If you could grow and blossom my spirits like the thickest red rose

Nearest to me

Pedals

If you could roll as quick as I flow my homemade lyrics

With just the beat of my tongue tease

Petals

If you could light up my life like the breath of the sun does yours

And

The colors of my soul could soar like the artistry that flows from your

vine

Pedals

If you could spin my life with the breeze

Just a spinning and spinning

Quickly

Petals

If you could open to the waste of my life like you open to the bees

And

Let me spill forth my nectar on your leaves

Pedals

Petals

I would be free

Jamel Latria Daralea

In Death

I am singing in my sleep

Memorizing poetry in my sleep

Exercising and building up a sweat in my sleep

Crying in my sleep

Forever thinking in my sleep

I am ever awake even in my sleep

The moment is all there is

In death, I will sleep a deep complete sleep

Something Hilarious

You learn from your mistakes

A blemish is not a flaw

A pain is but a pleasure

Your enemy is your friend

An empty belly is actually full

We are all created equal

All good will come to those whom wait

Give offerings to receive blessing, do not give, and hope to receive

Jamel Latria Daralea

Born to die, die to be born

Everyone and everything in this world is born and dies

Man woman and child

Beast and environment

Continually passing through birth and death

The breath of life, the last breath, the cycle miraculous and beautiful

The elaborate wonders of it all occurring

The thought on how and when

Is truly grand

How though that of all this wealth

The environment

Having beast and being man

How could man reverse the plan?

With his ragged and savage insight, his intelligence only ignorance

His mind with his hands can damage

Like many paints tossed on sheet and called art, unappealing

Man can now create breath and take it away

Once the throes of death was without pain, without guilt, without shame

Once upon a time, I am sure

That in death the clouds would glide you into the heavens and the sun
would not burn but soothe

Now the clouds are gray, the sun is on fire, and we have storms ahead

Greedy

I hunger and thirst to only be fulfilled

I wish to be fulfilled which brings substantial filling

Why is this a sin?

Because, fulfillment comes from within the wanting and wishing is greedy, you will conceive more than you need

Why must your cup overflow? When it could be shared and all thirst quenched.

Why cannot your belly rumble for the depletion of another's swollen belly of hunger and pain?

Greediness comes from wanting, why must your cup overflow only to waste, this is a sin

Erudition

Erudition is the key.

I feed my mind more than my body.

Knowledge allows me to grow fastidious and elite in any area I please.

I live in more places than one. I am more things than real life can allow me.

Anything that touches the heart and reaches the soul, but utmost frees my mind and enchants new things in me.

Erudition is the key.

Religion

Sin

The wet, rich, Earth springs forth around me

Covering my naked body like a dark sheath

Protecting me from the Sun.

Everything gliding tenebrously around my body like a quilt.

The lively smells of leaves are ever so sweet

Imprinting inside my nostrils a dewy perfume

Discreet though enchanting

The last thing my senses will remember before I am engulfed in a realm

of selfish dark creatures.

Graceful is thy walk; lazy is thy run, Sin

You leap though sly into my presence with swamp like eyes, dark and

murky, digging deeper into me than your

Mouth can dine my flesh

Sin is leaving within me scars of hunger

The abuse on my life

Is that I might search for my soul

My soul runs from me, as I am close to you Sin

I hunger

The anguish hunger for life, Sin

Love

Serenity

The anguish hunger to be like you, Sin

See how you see deep into me

My blood screams for you, Sin

Screams out the passions that lay dormant

You release the drum like entity that lay buckled under my angelic
hold, Sin

It beats against your fangs, Sin

Your

Griping jaws, Sin

Your

Thumping tongue, Sin

And

You like it

My Lord what must I do, that I am confused on what to choose

Each way I loose

When I reach for your comfort and I long for Sins vulgarities

Which latch tight to my impurities, and trick me into ease

Sometimes it seems the same, good and evil

Evil and good

Serves the same purpose it seems

Confusion and more confusion

"*I*"

God said, "I!"

Devil said, "I!"

Competition of two conflicting egos

Agnostic

Do I believe?

Is there a higher entity I wish to grab?

Something more beautiful, more intelligent

Engulfed in more peace than anyone

Anything

Floating high above the clouds

Passing us by like airy drip drops

When I call out in anguish

When I sing songs of praise or mourning

It is to a being

Infested in me by the creativity of this lonely discontent world perhaps

Or the curiosity of a pessimist beating at the mind

Painfully

Or

Is it my intuition that tells me to look above and smile?

After all the tease

Mockery

Hatred

Carried on daily

The world with no meaning unless we can be above all

But

All was created for us... not to rule but to love and cherish

When I sit serene in my secret vision

Hymns flow around my head in notes bouncing unknown choruses off

my throat

Tears of joy not noticeable to me run like the Red Sea down my cheeks

My eyes swell with life only to dehydrate into the clouds

I become the character in many books

A closer look

I am the conclusion in the beginning

The beginning

I am the beginning

Words come to me in many languages and great imagination

For I see myself as many and all

And

All hover around my heart

Finding a thick place to harvest immense beauty

Instilling in my soul a right of passage and direction

I cherish this entity

What created me is in me

Peace

Love

Direction

My heart is resting snug with my soul

I believe

In

Me

Church

We are laughing (haha)

We are smiling (smile)

Eyes closed and dreaming

Swaying and thinking (Moving body back and forth)

Feet thumping on the floor, shoulders popping

Necks knocking

Hands together and clapping (clap)

Reminiscing to this music

It is playing and the drums are beating

They beat and beat

The bass is strong

The rhythm so rhythmic

The sounds uplifting

Energizing

Mesmerizing

Church

Church II

What is a church if it is not a home?

A home is warm and welcoming, not judgmental and conflicting

What is a church if it is only for the Catholics, the Baptist, the

Pentecostal, the Orthodox, the Jewish, the Muslim, the Hindu, the

Protestant?

Those are not church but religions

Religions with views to confuse and use (let us not hide from the truth)

Reaching as far as the heart, ridiculing the soul and latching hold to the

spirit

Divine the essence that is perceived on, when to, where to, what to do,

how to receive this higher glory

Confusion on what to choose, how to abide by, how to worship, when to

worship, which name to call and how to call it, he, she, it, scientific

theories, how to pray when to pray, fast, rest, slave, master

Once a positive, now preposterous disaster, that, those, them Religions

Church is a home

Solid, warm and welcoming

Church is a people

Solid, strong, and glorious

Church is warm, welcoming and embracing

My Lord

My Lord

Look what you have done for me

I am like one with thee

My Lord

Your heavenly sounds caressing me

Warmth burns my heart

Tender in its cradle

No light is brighter

Than the one, you have shown me

My Lord

Look what you have done for me

I am like one with thee

I feel so free like the leaves on the trees

I can see your smile stretching across the sky miles and miles

The shine in your eyes painting the smooth sky with surprise

My Lord

My Lord

My Lord

Praise

I watch them crying praise

Pathetically, whining like dogs to their master

Who gives them no reply and if they can hear, they do not understand

For this entity says it is not the voice to hear but the essence of love to embrace

Do they hear?

Do they really feel?

Do they understand?

"Where are you, who are you, what are you?" I ask these questions in my head and I judge them with my eyes.

I watch them disgusted

Eve

Who am I you ask?

Sometimes I ask myself the same questions.

It seems that I am many, of that I am sure.

My memories are sad ones

My lives are of pain and more pain.

I am of honor and dishonor

I am a happy woman, sometimes a scorned woman. I am creature and

beast. I am to lay and be laid.

Too many years it seems that my body has been ravaged.

For no moment in time have I felt of anything or anybody except when

it was only Adam, our paradise, and I.

Now it seems

I feel warmth just as great, when I am with you.

However, it is only a beginning to this life.

I may get a chance to start over again.

Maybe

Life has seemed to evolve before my very eyes and still life is the same

for me.

To rely on the past and its torment for too long will dry me out.

Moreover, now I feel love once again.

Fear of god

Why fear what is to protect and teach us?

Why fear what we are?

We are created with thirsty hearts and loins- each alike because one

speaks to the other-and, spirits of souls not in our grasp but on hold for

a future yet untold

Nevertheless, God gives us free to blossom and wither, fall and then

blossom again

Even if some shall, blossom but thirst and some shall bloom and starve

Although, most will fall and never blossom again

For it is the confusion of the fear that is

Instead of the love it should be

Why fear, when I would dream to communicate and embrace physically

this entity

I do not hear nor see

Issues

Jamel Latria Daralea

Motherhood

Motherhood is

Grace

Grace I wish

Fate

Fate maybe

A premonition

Less than likely

A decision

Not always

A smile a few times

Proud

A struggle for sure

A dimple in your life

Guaranteed

We can relate at least most of the human race

A good and bad date

A rape of the heart from the very start

Maybe a bliss that is quickly distinguished

Divorced and split

The crying and anguish

Wingless beings given to us

To devour our time

Entangle our minds

And then

They grow, grow, and never stop growing

We are broke

Privacy stole

Respect outgrown

Skip away

Skip away

Skip

Skip

Skip away

In a daze or the worst way

That is motherhood

It should

It would

It is

However, at times it is good

In the silence of the night

When the moon is half-bright

And

The smiles that embrace the Childs face

Their sleeping eyes and fetal positioned figures

Indenting their shadows into the covers

The sweet smell of their childish sweat

And the silky glow of their slobber sliding into the pillow

Ah,

Reminds you of the beauty

You and your mate

One lousy date

One long wait

To the end of a stressful day

The making love that you made

Or

The quick fuck

You were played

In the roughness of the sheets

Lubricated, noisy flesh

The orgasm you did not meet with his

The nut he easily seeded in your womb

The egg that flourished in your tomb

Motherhood

The father

Who is quickly bothered

Who by his feet is a sneak

Out the door without a peek

Emotionally staining

Agitating your beauty

Your ego dismantled

Self-esteem bleached clean

Motherhood

Stretched out

Fatback

Paddy whack

Give a dog a bone

Over weight

Out of shape

Extra stock in exercise tapes

Motherhood

Though

At times, it is good

When the bubble bath is hot and sensual

And

The music plays ecstasy

And

The movie can be heard and seen

Without mommy

This

And

Mommy that

Mommy replacing the first name

All the same

Motherhood

Really misunderstood

A gift of meaning

It should

Of sharing

It would

Of pleasing

It is

Of giving and not receiving

Only the notion you have succeeded in a creation

Motherhood

It is good

My Love Child

Baby you are my love child

Everything I want to be

Everything I need to be

I hope you will take from me

You are apart of me

You are my destiny

I look in the mirror and I see your face

Your tears misplaced

Your heart is swelling from my negligence

But

Everything I do is for you

Without my negligence

We have no future

You carry your book bag like a suitcase

Ready for a work day

Suppose to be school day

There is no time to play

Or

Talk about the day

Homework before everything

Your eyes are closing

Your thoughts are

Same o same

My feet are hurting from working overtime

And

My mind is bugging

Picking up college classes with our extra dimes

Childcares costly

Government's bossy

On the weekends, we try to fit activities in

But

We do not go anywhere

Because we're tired from the weekday

I am sorry baby

I am sorry baby

My little men

My little lady

In a growing world

Giving you dress shoes and high heels

You have no chance to be a kid

Wearing ties at five

Stockings at nine

I love you

You are my future

Mothers Pain

She lay there

Face plump and pale

Eyes wide and dry

She lay there

Her breast thick with milk

Leaking out of her like tears

She lay there

Her stomach stretched and retched

Wide over her still beautiful thighs

Covering her shrinking, bleeding beat up lily

She lay there thinking about future years

She lay there

With a smile on her face

Her child lying in her arms wide eyed

She lay there

Blessed

Mothers' pain

Mothers gain

Jamel Latria Daralea

Joys of My Life

The joys of my life

Are the consistent strife

It is the comfort of my body

Pressed lucratively with my burning shadow, the sunlight mirrors on

my automobile window

It is the forever-saddened twin in my mirror

In which I once saw gracefulness within

A little peace if the world would let it show me a wide grin

The joys of my life

Is my anger smacked thickly across my face like pomade

It shines

It is when you look at me, you see it and shudder

Even in the smile and the glitter in my eyes

Yet you still wonder

For my eyes are blank, distant in space

My head is high

I shy away

And

You still wonder

You wonder if I have a friend

The joys of my life

Is when a Nobody becomes somebody

Because in my life

There are too many nobody'

Idiot

Liar

Cheater

Jargon

Charlatan

Deceiver

Drunk

Impetuous

Tragicomic

Imbecile

Thief

Creep

Racist

Broke

A real idiot

Standard

I don't know if I found him

Or

He found me

But

We are together now

And

More than anything, I am enjoying this small moment

When I can look over him in silence

He is what society calls standard

He is a middle-aged man

With a distant

Separated family of the sorts

Seems I could get no lower

This is way below my standards

But oh well he is a man

He is not a poster boy

I am starving for his attention kind of man

Nah

He is a regular man

With an accent

Seems decent enough

Very honest

I think

He is tall

Medium build

More belly than I would wish

And

He is hairy

His face

Hmm

Accentuated with black olive beauty

Blemish free, unlike me

Boyish features

And his eyes

Oh am I falling?

His eyes are haunting

Dark like marbles

Like a deer's eyes

Captivating

Endless, ever so endless

And calling me

Society calls him standard

Jamel Latria Daralea

Black Man, Brown Man

He who is alone, with no one to consider, may give the reigns of his grief
a tug too many times

And his reigns will never fall they are a barrier most of all

His eyes pour forth a stream of tears, which flow down his cheeks to his
breast

Breast, which are covered in scars beaten by his own hands

He is an actor

A rapper

A singer

An athlete

He is a businessperson

A well dresser

His stride is one of many

His strength is over coming

His voice asserts a tone so mournful

At times, you would wish to hold onto him

A tone of terror

Rebelling, at times repelling

One must hold a shield

A tone of power

A tone of fatherly love

He knows his language, but he confuses people from the outside

He enjoys the sound of his own voice and is one with his demeanor

He has nothing in his head.

His body is his keeper

His protector

His destroyer

He is a man

A black man, a brown man

A confused man

STD

Sexually Transmitted Disease

I didn't give it to her

She gave it to me

I did not give it to him

He gave it to me

Please

I said, use protection, he said he did

(When you both are finished doing your thing)

Where is it?

Where is what?

What do you mean what? Where is the condom, I do not see it.

Get it from a man; pass it on to a man

Get it from a woman pass it on to a woman

One will give it and one will borrow it

I am still stuck on the absence of his condom

Why?

What was he thinking? Could he be so trustworthy?

Or

Is he desperate and lonely?

I could be burning

I have burned before

That is what occurs with lust and action

Before thinking

My already disappointed flesh angry

This is why I am alone

What will he give me I am already scorched

My scorched flesh hibernating disease for eternity

He may receive

I look at him with disbelief

No condom and limp meat

I hope it was good

Fool

Life Is Bare

When life is bare it is sweet

It is beautiful and honest

It is love

Bare is the softness of the smooth skin

The beauty illuminating from within

The thinking and thought

The essentials of tender love

That only we can give

Pure as an angel's day

Is what we are

Is what we should be

And

Then he comes

Hard and rough like the dry bark of a tree

Mind as empty and sly as a donkey

How he detains you

With his stinking mouth

Wet and tarter tongue

Lying lizard of the swamp

With prying eyes on you or a few

He comes to make you gullible

To cause you unstable

Unbearable

He comes to tighten your skin

To make you greedy and arrogant

To want and wish

To loose your patience and therefore your blessings

To cause you pain

For your closeness to his bulky frame

He comes and takes away the light and beauty in your life

The once sweet and soft, the deepest joy

Is now hard and lost and full of anger

Beauty

Beauty

Beauty

Beauty

Oowee

Baby, baby

Look at sista thick

Thick thighs

Hazel eyes

Cheeks high

Azz

Hmm

Spreading her hips wide

Damn

Look at her sway from side to side

Now that's my kind

Big breast

Cleavage

In the chest

Thick chocolate bitch

Catch that fish

Catch it

Oowee

Baby, baby

Hmm

Yeah

See she got them lips

Lick

Hmm

Thicker than thick

Full as shit

Them lips to wrap around my dick

With the quickness

Nut all over her juicy lips

Gum it baby

Gum this big

Fat

Dick

Skull her ass 'til I cum

Hmm

Juicy thick bitch

We want up in that shit

She got that video bod

Young

Fine

Hard

Damn

Sit her bodacious ass on my lap

Slap

Tap-tap

That ass

Big O booty

Cutey

Dig all up in her fat

Deep

Pussy

Rub and suck her clit

Or

Is

Until she squirts and shit

Who's your daddy bitch?

Damn

Slide my dick between her breasteses

Hmm

Juicy thick

Booty

Bitch

Hoe

Fish

Beauty

Damn

Beauty

They noticed her eyes

Nothing inside

See

They did not see her smile

White

Fresh and

Clean

They did not see her style

Conservative

Fine

Mean trend

Wild

They did not hear her talk

Manners

Proper

Educated

No Ebonics bulk

They did not see her ride

Expensive

Up to date

All work

No play

They did not

Uh huh

They did not

See her beauty was in the hips

How they could handle it

Her beauty was in the sway

Her lips

The way her mouth could be dealt with

Her beauty was in the word bitch

Characterization of a today woman

Definition of a dog

They did not

Uh huh

They did not

They saw there nut on her gut

They saw her ass fucked

Rough

They saw her tits

Exposed

Shaking

Jiggling

They saw her lips swell

Sucking on there long

Thick

Penises

They did not see the college education

They did not see a sister

A daughter

They did not see a perfect woman

They did not

Uh huh

They did not

Beauty

Beauty

Meow

Beauty

There definition

Of

Beauty

Our breakdown of self-respect

Our breakdown of self-love

Our inventor of self-disrespect

Our inventor of self-hate

Creator of suicidal lust

Expectance

Acceptance

A sad lesson

Old suggestions

A wicked revelation

A new generation

Beauty

Jamel Latria Daralea

Come here baby, come here

Hmmm

Come here baby

Come here

Hmmm

Come on baby

I said,

Come here

Hmmm, Ya

You see that baby

Yeah

You see it getting bigger baby

Come here

Come closer girl

Bring your sweet cheeks

It likes you

Don't be scared

Hmmm

I said,

Get your ass over here

Girl

It'll be good to you

It'll just take a few

Minutes of your attention

All your mommas' pension

Come here baby

I'm gonna be your daddy now

We gonna love each other

Take care of one another

Don't you want to be my friend?

To the end

I know you do

Come here baby

Come here

Hmmm

That's right

A little closer

And closer

And closer

Hmmm

Lay your head on my thigh

Go ahead

Get comfortable

Hmmm

Kiss it baby

Kiss it

Don't be scared

Don't be shy

(Man laughing)

Damn I'm high

Don't cry baby

Dry ya eyes

Hmmm

Go ahead kiss it

Kiss it girl

Hmmm yeah

See

Now kiss it harder

That's the way it's suppose to be

(Girl whimpers)

Shut up girl, ok I'm sorry baby girl

Touch it

Hmmm yes

Touch it!

Come here bitch!

I ain't your bitch

Oh, you my bitch and some other things to

I ain't your bitch, fool!

Oh, you gonna be my bitch today

See I remember you

How little and cute you use to be

Your fat chubby cheeks sucking on everyone's meat

Just like, I told you to

Bringing in much loot

You listened to me

A big happy family

You, my homies, and me

Come here, bitch

I ain't your bitch

You my bitch and some other things to

You gonna do what I say like before 'cause you owe me

I took care of you

I brought you in when your momma sold you out

Sipping on the pipe lost in the crack

Ya you owe me

Where your daddy at

Hmmm

Yeah you remember this package

Go ahead lick your lips

He's your friend

Give it a kiss

Lend your hand

Hmmm

I can still feel those hot fleshy cheeks

Your throat choke

Your whimpering voice

Hmmm so sweet

So young

All for me

Come here bitch

I ain't your bitch

I ain't sucking your dick

Damn prick

You had me before

But

You won't make me a whore

I can walk out that door

I won't come back no more

Oh you not leaving bitch

Your momma ain't paid up shit

See look at it this way your the only way I get paid

And if I don't get paid

Then you're my sex slave

You fifteen, it's been a hell of a lot of years

I doubt your momma even cares, or you wouldn't be here

Hmmm

Today is your lucky day

'Cause I am gonna devirgin your tang

And some other things

Now come here bitch

Before you get your head split

Hmmm

Yeah do what I taught ya

Dedicated to that child sold to the streets for a small piece of misery

To that made to be hoe, whore, slut, and wish to be queen of the streets

Dedicated to that masculine creature Jack be reaper want to be pimp

That crack and dust keeper

Dedicated to the lost

Racial Tending

Racist

It is not that I do not like your color

Well maybe I do not like your color

Nevertheless, you wear it

I do not

I mean you all look the same

Do the same things

Act the same way

White Power

Damn you

Damn you

Black boy

Black girl

Reparations you scream

With your killing machines

An army in every hood

The gun and drugs lessens your numbers the way it should

Damn you

Damn you

All you do is complain

And

Then ask for gain

In all your ignorance and shame

Damn you

Damn you

With your unintelligent slang

Your rappers and gangs

The bass

You are the last race

As we say, y'all are a pile of human waste

Damn you

Damn you

Damn beggars

Bootleggers

Whores

Damn ugly beast across our shores

Polluting our schools with all your Ebonics' bull

Asking for a second chance

A free hand

Bastard kids

Damn you

Your people can be happy only if you are cursed, downtrodden, and kept in chains.

Servitude to cotton plentitude is your virtue

How you make us laugh

That love blinds you

You love humanity, but it does not love you back

It does not want you

I want to scream for suicide

I want to kick your asses but I cannot

Damn all of you

For making me scream horrible things to my white ancestors

I see my people and I feel shame

What have we gained from owning slave chains?

Damn you, if I could choose I would not be you or me

Equality

Who says either of us are free

Black Power

Did you say damn me?

No! DAMN you!

Pale boy

Pale girl

With your ringlets and blue eyes

Damn you

Damn you

Lying ass governments

Prostitution covenants

Drug makers and dealers

Race and culture stealers

Damn you

Damn you

Nosey heathens

Profiteers from deceiving

Pedophile fathers of the church hanging crosses down between your shirts

Breaking families with vulgar deception

Your unholy perceptions

Damn you

Damn you

Incest plaques

Owner of slaves still today for the green of dirty bills

Blood money

You are the NIGGERISH population

Ignorance the definition

You give us that name

By far, you are the nigger

Damn you

You make me laugh

You make me scream and cry

You make me want to kick your ass

And

I can

In the open skirts of the ghetto

The no grass or trees

Just potholes

In the drugs and swain of a liquors gain

I cry to my ancestors

That sold so boldly

My long ago family

Instead of fighting to protect

Like the proud Ethiopiawit

And no gain

Just like me for centuries, Africa and I have felt the pain

The blood that flowed on its Eden

To supply you pale with ethnic seasons and build your country from

fear of running

For the torture of your devilish look, and the smoking bullets in your

guns

We mistook for hell

You have no excuse and nothing to gain

So stop complaining

Damn you

We live on your humanity

Wicked

Incapable of fair benefits

Tricked

If I could choose

I would not be you

I would be me with equality

Back in my black beautiful Africa from the beginning

Remember

Remember, remember, and remember

How can we remember or forget

A past we do not know

However, the world is destined to show us

Remember, remember, and remember

But

I do not

And

No matter how much you try to remind my thoughts

Of memories ashore Africa's dark body

I do not remember

Even I do not know

And

Neither did my ancestors know

But

Know of

Sure

Know just as much as you know of me

Dream, dream, and dream

But

I do not

At least not, what you would expect of my dreams

And

No matter how much you would try to crucify my mind

With starving and disease

With people unlike me

I am of the cultures, tribes, and lives, happy content lives

Permanently erased from Africa's land of many

I am a tourist

Just like you

A black different from the other blacks

And

Many other things I cannot explain

I cannot dream a dream I cannot remember

I cannot remember a dream I have yet to dream

Indignation

Growing up in a world that is of constant confusion

Watching as my people go from nothing to noticed, and something to not noticed

Yeah I know we were somebody but I do not know when

See my generations got more money to spend but nothing to show

We got fly clothes on our backs

Shoes on our feet

Grills clean and conditioned

Permed

Curled

Riches baby

It is all a joke

See because they do not know who they are or where they began

But then

I do not think they give a shit

Shit is life as they put it

Ya put it in and then ya put it out

Ya you live it as you make it

Disrespect, demean, and bleed

Ya got me

Oh, wait let us blame it on the white man

Uncle Sam

Green eggs and ham

Damn

Oh, wait lets blame them immigrants

Who through their suffering made their way across the way?

Oh, wait

No, it was my ancestors suffering

That brought them this way

So many things from us they take away

However, it is only today always a tomorrow

But then

We have had too many today's and tomorrow's

Nothing has changed

Not just in this land but overseas

You dig

I am not talking a hundred years ago, twenty years ago, and not even last year

Damn

I am talking about the seconds

Minutes

Hours

I am talking about today

Today that the lord has made

It's suppose to be a good day

When I say I am confused… you know this world

I am not speaking of anyone's world but the black mans

Cause

I am black

Stacked with a beautiful shade

Proud

I am of the first man and woman the Lord made

Ya, always that

And

That is my priority

That is the main subject

My first objection

My only real reflection

You dig

But

Today is the same shit that happened yesterday, and the day before that

and so on and so on

Ya know

See we live in the past

A past we don't know, ya we learn some things here and there, but we

don't know

See if we knew the past and the ass kicking, ass raping, ass kissing our

ancestors suffered

How they buffered their nails across one another

Bled and cried on one another

Sold their soul to protect and save one another

Here, here

The mentality is harsh

The reality is harsher

Let us swoosh back to the beginning...

See we have not been noticed, but portrayed

Today when we have made it, accomplished

We are called the house nigger

What the hell is a house nigger?

Damn

The sell out

The Oreo

Is that not a cookie?

And

Then the same copy us

Who have tried to dissolution are beauty and talent

Merely ruin us of what we are by adopting our ways and tarnishing

them into laughter

However, I must contribute the downfall of my brother and sister over

there

Over there

And

Damn everywhere

I look

To themselves and the other brother and sister around them

To say confused and abused and betrayed by the human race

How about our own belittlement

Hahaha

I am laughing now

Do da de do boo bop da le la

Would you like to go back...?

Home

Umm home to Africa

Africa that large, beautiful continent full of sickness and death

Where the people live day to day in a curse

Where the animals hide and the trees die and the grass withers away

And

The rain refuses to come

No rainbows

You hear the mothers cry

Fathers and sons die

Sisters are deprived

Of their womanhood at such an early age

Oh not just deprived but ill figured

Politically unstable

Personal suicide

You dig

Would you like to take that journey with me?

Where the people we see

Do not exactly place in our database

Where the people get our last change

Instead of our broke, illiterate, crack headed, HIV communities here
receive

The ones who know us only through their suffering to compare with
ours

Come on

Let us take that journey

Home

Where we are not welcomed with open arms or smiles of love and
acceptance

Let us go home where we can sit at a doorstep and no one will hear our
knocks

Let us go home where our ancestors, ancestors wallop around in tears
soaking up the dry dirt

For they don't know their destination nor their beginning

Where our ancestors have come back in spirit to be slapped into pain in
their after life

Let us go home...

Where not even a syllable we can recognize but the wiggly smiles on
their face

Or

The stuck frowns to take a smiles place

Or

Maybe a stare of amazement

Would you like to go home?

To the place where you think, your last name resides

You are so lost

What is wrong, did you see a nose like yours?

Hahaha

Or

Maybe some eyes wide and cunning

Hahaha

Or

Maybe it was a woman that caught your libido when it was at its end

Or

Maybe it was the soft accent coming out of that man

Or

Maybe it was the dusty streets

Full of incense and the lyrical beat and charm

The soulful dance, the food, the romance

Damn

I know

It is hard

Did it ever cross your mind those faces you see

The sad ones

The angry ones

Even the happy ones

Are all around you where you're at now

Na

I know you did not

See our ancestors cry for us, though they blind us with their rivers of

sympathy

Oh man I'm laughing and crying

I am ashamed

I am mortified

By the existence of imbeciles that are to be my sisters and brothers

Cousins

Uncles

Aunts

I am sick of the bloodline that flows from you to me and me to you

Damn

Do da de do boo bop da le la

Laughing but not ashamed

I am not ashamed to be called

A nigger that is

Hurt maybe but not ashamed

See the word nigger is spoken from the niggers themselves

It does not have my name in its definition

The word nigger is to contribute to their not having self respect

To contribute to there blood line of Satan himself

Who could not dig the rules but create the ones he wished to follow

And

That my friend is why he wallows deep beneath my feet burning slowly

But

I do hurt

I hurt because I am human

But

The hurt comes from my heart reaching out to slap a brother or sister

who looks like me

Whose mother and father looks like, mines

My hurt comes from deep into my feet, which controls the stutter of

energy it feels

When it wishes to kick into the soul of my own people whom lash at my

dignity

And

Show me no respect

My own people

Nigga this

And

Nigga that

I do not think so

What happened to the brother and sisters we use to be?

Please

I am hurting

The people who will look down on me when they come from the worst

The people who will burn me with their starving eyes

Gang up on me with their twirling tongues

And

Laugh into my face as if we are one

Wow

I am laughing

To be called a nigger by harder naps than mines

Their skin so dark it is blue

Or

Maybe those ones with noses stretched from ear to ear

Their foreheads pushing out their eyes

Or

Wait

Hurt by them tall, slender beauties

With milky brown skin

Damn

And

Those afro curls to brush against their faces and fall upon there

eyelashes

Damn

And

Those black jewel eyes we wish to look into and swim

Damn

Ignorant they are

Ignorant

That we could treasure there pure existence

That we could treasure there country

There strength and there views

There dignity and self respect

And

Then they could walk upon the dirt that my great grandparents

suffered to achieve respect

How can they say they do not know us?

But

They are we more than anyone is

I am laughing because I am pissed

I am tired of all the nonsense

I am tired of being...

APE

MONKEY

DARK SAVAGE

NIGGER

BLACK

AFRICAN

I am tired of the movies bullshit

People slashed by the whip for some producer to go home and joke about

Ya, the actor is paid, but the mind is betrayed

Their minds are being raped and therefore they are raping the minds and hearts of all that

Are content

I am tired

Do da de do boo bop da le la

We went from strong, beautiful, creatures in the most beautiful place on Earth

AFRICA

The chosen place God had his prints on

Eden is there hidden under the caked dirt and the dead bodies and the old souls of

Yesterday

I want to be free Dammit

I want to be free from the stories that destruct our minds

Which in time have constructed our ignorance

When our thoughts become passionate to succeed and live

I will smile every time I see my peoples face

I want that kind of proud pain to surge in me

I want people to look at us as God did

As we are precious to the almighty

For no one is like us

We hold the gifts of heaven

We are the singers at God's gate

The voices that animate the heavens with peace, joy

And

Dance

We are the designated authors to complete a mans journey

We are the strength that has kept Satan occupied

We dance on his toes

For he can not get between are force and into heaven

For we were created in God's righteousness

So therefore, we hold the power to be in him

We are black for the sun loves to rest against are skin

The stars like to shine us with jewels

We are black because it is to remind the world

That once the earth was black and God created light to see the beauty

he had created

This Earth will be black again

For the dark is everywhere

I am laughing

Because now I am content once again

Let me dance

ABOUT THE AUTHOR

Jamele Latria Daralea is an up and coming author.

She is a young, talented writer and artist.

Speaking sensuality to the heart, life's misfortunes and bargains to the mind and serenity to the spirit, and sometimes speaking forth those vulgarities we hide.

To dare you to open her books and view the detail of her words, seep deep into her thoughts... would ask you to open a door to a dream, a fantasy, history, a complex of curiosity and truth, and find yourself living it.